With love to Frank.

First, you gave Phoebe and me a lifetime of wonderful memories.
Then, you gave me the encouragement and support to share them.

www.mascotbooks.com

The Famous Phoebe of Long Island: Phoebe's Adventures at Sailors Haven

©2021 Jean Derespina. All Rights Reserved. No part of this publication may be reproduced, stored in a retrieval system or transmitted in any form by any means electronic, mechanical, or photocopying, recording or otherwise without the permission of the author.

For more information, please contact:
Mascot Books
620 Herndon Parkway, Suite 320
Herndon, VA 20170
info@mascotbooks.com

Library of Congress Control Number: 2021904082

CPSIA Code: PRT0521A
ISBN-13: 978-1-64543-936-3

Printed in the United States

The Famous Phoebe of Long Island

Phoebe's Adventures at Sailors Haven

Jean Derespina

Illustrated by Amelina Jones

I'm Phoebe, and I am the luckiest dog in the world. I'm lucky because out of all the puppies in the shelter, I got picked by the nicest family. They love me very much.

"Do you want to go for a boat ride?" my new mom, Jeana, whispered in my ear. Even though I was just a puppy and I didn't know what a boat ride was, I was so excited! My tail wiggled and wagged beyond my control, and I licked her face.

Frank, my dad, said, "Let's go, Phoebe. We're going to Sailors Haven."

We all got on our boat.

We rode off into the Great South Bay. I must admit, I was more than a little scared at first, but Jeana held me close while Frank drove.

Soon, I realized riding in a boat felt just like when I stuck my head out of a car window, only the breezy feeling was all over me—right down to my tail! What fun!

After a delightful boat ride across the bay, we arrived at a marina, where there were lots of other boats. Once we settled in, my vacation adventures began.

Before I even got off the boat, I was surrounded by people and puppies. A big puppy named Alex said, "Welcome to Sailors Haven." Two tiny, pretty pups named Delilah and Higgins were bouncing up and down barking, "Nice to meet you, Phoebe!" Alex, Delilah, and Higgins became my first vacation friends.

Jeana and Frank took me for a walk through the Sunken Forest. I could tell by the many smells that there were lots of animals around. I saw squirrels, birds, and something I had never seen before. A long, skinny animal that didn't have legs or paws wiggled right by us! It was a snake. All these animals, even the snake, smiled at me and welcomed us into the forest.

We turned a corner and came to a small clearing. I spotted something wonderful. I thought it was the biggest dog I had ever seen. But it wasn't . . .

"Look, Phoebe, it's a deer!" Frank said.

A deer!

She stood perfectly still and stared at me with big, beautiful, brown eyes. I think she was as surprised as I was.

We stared at each other until finally, she winked, and in a flash, she turned and ran into the woods. She ran so swiftly that her feet hardly touched the ground. I was sad because I didn't mean to frighten her away. I was hoping she could be my vacation friend, too.

It was the bluest water as far as I could see. Children were playing in the sand. People were swimming and walking along the shore.

"Look at the ocean, Phoebe!" Frank exclaimed. "Tomorrow we'll go to the bay where you can swim." I couldn't wait to learn about swimming!

We walked back to the boat, and soon, Jeana and Frank were eating dinner.

I looked toward the dunes and saw three deer eating dinner, too. One stopped and looked at me with her big, beautiful, brown eyes. She winked. It was the deer from the Sunken Forest!

This was my chance to become friends with her. But before I could convince Frank to take me for a walk, she was gone again.

Soon, it was dark, and we sat on the back of the boat together. I climbed into Jeana's arms and rolled onto my back. Boy, was I tired. What a delightful and adventurous day!

I looked up and saw millions of stars lighting up the sky. Jeana held me until my eyes closed.

The next day, Frank took me to the bay. I was glad to see my friend Alex was there. The bay water was much calmer than the ocean, so I didn't hesitate—I ran right in.

I found out I knew how to swim! Alex and I swam back and forth. We chased balls and swam in and out. After we enjoyed playing for a while, Alex and I swam back toward the shore.

Suddenly, a bird flew by. It had something in its mouth. "Look at me, Phoebe," the bird tweeted. "I caught a fish."

I dropped my ball and watched the bird with the fish in his mouth. Where was he going? Was he inviting me to have dinner with him?

I really wanted to find out, so I followed him. I ran and ran down the beach, trying to catch up to the bird with the fish in his mouth.

Then the bird with the fish in his mouth turned and flew over the bay. I stopped at the shoreline and watched the bird fly farther and farther away from me. Oh well. I guess I wasn't having fish for dinner.

When I couldn't see the bird anymore, I looked around. Where was everyone? Where was I? I was all alone, and I was really scared.

I looked back, and I could see Jeana and Frank running down the beach toward me.

"Phoebe! Phoebe, come back!" they were calling. Frank said to me, "Phoebe! What if you got lost?" I felt bad and promised myself I would never chase an animal again.

When we got back to the boat, I was so tired from all my swimming and running that I fell fast asleep even before the stars came out.

The next day, it was time to leave. All my vacation friends stood behind the boat to say goodbye.

"Goodbye!" barked Alex.

"See you soon!" said Higgins and Delilah, jumping up and down.

Two squirrels near the Sunken Forest waved to me.

A seagull flew overhead singing, "Caw, caw—nice to meet you, Phoebe."

And the bird that caught the fish called out to me, "Maybe next time we can have dinner together."

When the boat started to move, I took one last look at the dunes. Standing near the holly trees was the deer. She looked at me and winked one of her big, beautiful, brown eyes. "Come back and visit again soon, Phoebe!" she softly called out.

As we rode into the Great South Bay toward home, I looked back and lifted my paw to wave to all my new friends. Then, I licked Frank's face and wagged my tail at Jeana.

I am the luckiest dog in the world!

About the Author

Jean Derespina is a small business owner who writes marketing materials for her clients. In addition to her business writing, she has been a creative writer for many years, but this is her first published book. Jean and her husband, Frank, spent about twenty years boating on the south shore of Long Island. They often spent weekends or longer at the Fire Island National Seashore communities.

About the Illustrator

Amelina Jones is an illustrator with a passion for nature, tea, and stories. She works in traditional watercolor and ink, incorporating storytelling elements and emotions into her work. The gentle form of watercolor mixed with her unique, whimsical style creates illustrations that aim to enhance a story and bring it to life.

You can find more of AJ's work on her website amelinajones.com

If you want a dog as awesome as Phoebe, consider adoption.

Visit your local shelter to learn more.